# Psalmsongs

# Psalmsongs

## Gaya Aranoff Bernstein

an Arthur Kurzweil book
New York/Jerusalem

Cover art, *Jerusalem Hills,* by G.A. Bernstein.

Copyright © 2013 by Gaya Aranoff Bernstein
All rights reserved

AN ARTHUR KURZWEIL BOOK
11 Bond Street #456
Great Neck, NY 11021

First edition

Gaya Aranoff Bernstein
*Psalmsongs*

978-0-9855658-4-8

# Table of Contents

Preface
*vii*

---

Psalmsongs
*1*

---

Listing of Psalmsongs Based on Content
*153*

---

Index of First Lines
*155*

# Preface

When my youngest child was diagnosed with cancer, things changed. In the space of a few hours, my world became impossibly vulnerable, but surprisingly clarified. Things either mattered intensely, or not at all. Life mattered; prayer helped; reading *Psalms* calmed me down. I read *Psalms* in Hebrew and in English; I tried to make each psalm relevant to my torment. I hoped that my child's cancer cells would be like the ancient psalmist's enemies — impotent against the Almighty.

There are 150 psalms in the *Book of Psalms*. The language of biblical *Psalms* is beautiful, but can be cumbersome and difficult to absorb. These *psalmsongs* are psalms through the prism of my soul; they are interpretations rather than translations. I have attempted to make each one immediately accessible, while staying true to the corresponding biblical psalm. I've tried to convey the passion and timelessness of the psalmist's ancient angst, faith, resilience, and joy — the raw, unflinching depictions of the human condition, the intimate first-person conversations with an inconceivable God. Enemies still plague us; hope still sustains us. One does not have to be religious to try to make some sense of it all. There is comfort to be found in knowing that our modern questions are ancient questions, and that our common humanity can lead us to seek answers from the Creator.

— G.A. Bernstein

# Psalmsongs

# 1

to not get lost
to not get sidetracked
by the expected
by fad or fashion
of the time
to not keep up
with fools, sinners
others

to stay focused
on truth
your truth
God's truth
to yearn for it
day and night

to seek it
night and day
is to find
joy
truelife

like a sapling
near a stream
water for the taking
fruits in season
glistening leaves
growing
rooted

not blown away
a withered leaf
in autumn
an old newspaper
telling
ancient lies

# 2

stop the noise
Stop it
the idiocy of it
the propaganda
the screaming lying
headlines
Stop them
sightless powers
railing against God
and Israel

we believe in a God
we can't conceive of
but we know
we didn't create
ourselves

God must be amused
at their hubris
they are
out of
control

get real
editors  presidents
ministers  kings
your emperor
is naked
your castles
sand
your days
human
and God
is
not

# 3

O God
I am overwhelmed
by the demons
in my heart
at my heels
after me
taunting me
threatening me
aiming at me

but then I sense
You
here
with me

I get out of bed
lift my head
face my life
knowing You know
I'm surrounded

You get them
Kill those bastards
Break their teeth
Bless us

Selah

# 4

Just God
Answer me when I call
as You did
when things were tight
and I lost my will
to fight
Release me
again

pride-loving sycophants
yesmen
are there for me in my glory
for their glory

We know true love
You feel my tears
the fear and trembling
pounding in my heart
as I lie awake but

trust God
just God
who is
real
truth

I see You
in peace
more sweet
than spoils of war
You're here with me
I lie in bed
and safely sleep
alone

# 5

O my God I beg You
Hear me wail
see my tears
my cries my fears
O my God my King
my God I start my day
listening for You
waiting
knowing
You don't want evil men
boasting murderous slime
You don't want to look at them
You hate them

You want me
(deserving or not)
You want me
You know I'm waiting
listening always listening
for You
wanting You fearing You
dreaming of knowing You
dreaming of sitting in your palace
intimate old friends
Help me
I'm drugged
by their smooth talk
and twisted words
their wicked fat mouths
like open graves to me

You are my joy
and protection and
those who want to know You
know joy and protection and
song and love and
hope and kindness and
are blessed forever

# 6

O God don't punish me
don't be angry
have mercy
I am powerless
bereft
sick
spineless

Hear me
Heal me

O God
how long
can this go on
my soul aches
my terrified soul
burns

Free me
let my unworthy body
be   composed
I can't pray   sing
praise You
from my grave

every night
my eyes melt
my bed floats on tears
I have aged
I am drained

Pain, depart
God is with me
He hears me

your turn
to be scared

# 7

O God don't leave me
save me
enemies at my heels
are gaining ground
and I don't know
maybe I deserve
to be ripped to shreds
eaten alive by their lions

if I am guilty
let them
trample my soul
drag it in the dust
kill my name

You be the judge
test my honest heart
my brain
my guts

You be the judge
and test them too
see traps they set
the lying schemes
the pits they dig
for me

I'm trying to
come clean with them
be true to You
O God
expose their treachery
give them their due
as I praise You

# 8

Awesome Lord of all
I see You
in clods of earth
fertile beneath my feet
in clouds and moon
and stars and sky
soaring above my head
in suckling babies
who can't talk but will grow
to know You
tend Your sheep
and see Your mark
everywhere

why should You
care
about us

who are we
to be crowned
keepers
of Your earth
Your works
Your sheep and cattle
Your birds and fish
and oceans

O great God of all things
You care
we should

# 9

thank You God thank You God
thank You for this miracle
thank You with all my heart
anyone listening
I'm shouting singing
this miracle was wrought
by God
my enemies are in retreat
trapped in their own nets
drowning in their own slime
sliding into hell
who are they to have
presumed their own power
they control nothing
You rule
terrify them
Show them they die

You searched my heart
heard my case
judged justly
crushed my foes
each one of them
now toothless
swordless
impotent
wiped
out

infinite eternally
Your truth remains
resplendent
and though we are
ephemeral
we seek You   know
You are not deaf
to human cries
indefinitely

# 10

Where are You when I need You
when danger is steadfastly
there for me
where are You
whose side are You on
the evil do evil
and get away with it
thrive  prosper
they say You're
not there
not watching
not

Where are You
when they kill children
where are You
in famine and tsunamis
and war
where are You
when the old lady
is raped in her home
and he thinks no one sees

Show Yourself
the humbled can't breathe
when the air is full
of burning flesh
can't breathe
when lions
lick them
can't breathe
when they're drowning

they need to breathe
knowing You
see hear know
everything
knowing You
are just there
and just
here

# 11

In God I trust
Don't tell me to take wing
and fly away to safety
what's safety
when arrows can pierce my heart
in flight

In God I trust
to smash the
evil missiles
aimed at me and mine
under cover
of night

In God I trust
I trust in God
wherever He sits
in celestial glory
infinitely distant
infinitely intimate
to know my thoughts
to hear my pulse
race

I trust You God
to rescue me
Demolish all
who seek to harm
Rain sulfur on them
hellfire storms

I trust You God
to notice me
to know my love
to keep me safe

# 12

Help me God
I've lost my faith
in man

smoothtalkers
spouting lies
doublespeak

bloated by
false pride
convinced
they're their own
masters
convinced
they're ours

Master
of the universe
by Your word
Creator
of the universe
Speak for the weary
the speechless
the humbled
the muted by
life

Your works are Your words
visible in sterling purity
to those not blinded
by their own hot air
and engulfed
in fog

# 13

O God
I can't take this much longer
where are You
come out
come out
wherever You are
I can't take this
much longer
Help me

how much longer
can I take this
I can't plan
I'm running
on empty
bereft of ideas
my enemies swift
I see death

look at me
wherever You are
See me
I'm falling
I can't take this
much longer
O show me a light
that my eyes can find
shine on me now
See me

if I die
they'll think they won
they'll dance on my grave
if I live
I'll sing and praise
my God
the only One

# 14

they say God is dead
then they do as they please
but God sees
everything

He sees them
sit down to dinner
blood on their hands
meat in their teeth
laughing
victorious
as we mourn

we cry
they chew
devouring us
oblivious
to our pain
and God's
presence

He hears us
He sees them
He remembers
everything

we'll get out of this
alive
as God lives

# 15

who gets You
good God
who gets
to be near
Yourspace
to reach Your
mountaintop
paradise  utopia
nirvana  eden
wherever
You are
who gets eternal
soulpeace

> prepare
> be there
> with inner life
> in synchrony
> with outer life
> in thought
> in speech
> in deed
>
> be there with love
> be there with fear
> of One
> the only God
> then sure of foot and steadfast
> face steep inclines
> and climb

# 16

Stay close
You're mine

You're the source
of any good
coming my way

I've inherited You
the boundless wealth
of You
my parents
grandparents
and greats
earned You
and now You're
mine

Help me
guard my legacy
from raiders who
find it worthless
toss it out
raise their glasses
of blood
in empty victory

forgotten
they bequeath
dust

Blessed God
be with me
eternally
guide me rock steady
suffuse me with joy

I know You were
I know You are
I know that You
will be

# 17

hear me
listen to my thoughts
You know me inside out
I can't deceive
You

You read my heart
all night all day
You know I err
again
and yet I come
to You and cry
Forgive
at least I come to You
O that man   O that I
could pass Your tests
and always do what's right
I try and fail
I fail to try
have mercy

don't use my foes
their weaponry
to mete out punishment
surround me now
with clouds of love
just hide me now
protect me

they lurk like lions
proud and poised
to pounce and make their kill
they have no clue
they're just  Your tools

when my time comes
I want to die fulfilled with years
and progeny
I need more time
to purify my soul
my deeds  for You

# 18

I know my King
my rock my source
my strength
thank God
I live

I know You hear
my silent screams
when terror grips
at night
when I lie crouched
in chains in pain
in caves
pursued
You're there

in earth and wind
and fire and hail
and lightning thunder
clouds
You shake your cherubs
from the sky
and angel armies
rally to my aid

unbound by miracle
released
I flee  I'm out  I'm free
and armed by You
I soar and fly
leave enemies
in my wake

and if they call me
shepherd boy
or call me Israel's king
they know I bow
they know I serve my God
my God alone

# 19

the sky tells Your story
Your glory speaks
in orbits   planets
night and day
in webs of
space and time
sublime
the heavens express
Your will

each morning in joy
the sun like a groom
leaves its chamber
to start the day
with warmth uncontained
it leaps cross the sky
and radiates heat
light

Your light Your word
are gifts to us
eternally
we have to see
Your constancy
and symmetry
infinity

if only I
could stay the course
that You have set for me
and steep myself
in truth and love
and fear as You dictate
my soul enriched
would overflow

so guide my heart
my head my lips
to sing Your song
and heed You

# 20

when times are hard
and you are scared
and need and cry
My God! Hear me!
may He

remember when you sang to Him
reached out to Him
with thanks and praise
when times were good

may He
feel your pleading soul
suffuse it with joy

Others gird in armor
find strength in
guns and tanks
or see salvation
by the hands of
man
but metal melts
and metal twists
and man is clothed
in flesh

We know true power
lies in You
we speak Your name
we know You hear
and You renew
the strength of man
so he can stand
to live

# 21

I, mere king,
hail You my King
this victory is Yours
You read my lips
my silent plea
for life
I prayed
to win this deadly war
You fought for me
and won

a crown of answered prayers
swirl around my head
like golden leaves
encircling me
my path is strewn
with light

We asked to live
and here we are
eternally alive
 *Daveed melech Yisrael*
 *chai chai vekayam!*
 David king of Israel
 immortal Israel's king!
we're bound to You
in war and peace
and trust
that those who
plot our death
cannot escape Your reach

You'll seek and find them
wipe them out
obliterate their seed
while we
your loyal subjects
praise You
singing   joyous
safe

# 22

why have You left me
my God
my God so far away
and out of reach
more distant than a morning star
so mute all night
and deaf to all my cries

with mother's milk
for centuries
I learned to call to You
in hunger and in need
to trust the flow of
holy manna
from above

though I am just
an undeserving worm
in pain

come closer now
and hear the howling dogs
the lions roaring in the dark
come see my courage
melt like scalded wax
my fragile bones
exposed and parched
my garments strewn about

come feed me now
and clothe  protect
and shelter me and nourish me
and look at me and be with me

I sense that You are
somewhere  here
and that You know
my heart and care
and that it matters to You
that I serve and pray
and praise

# 23

You lead  I'll follow
and lack nothing

cushion my falls
softly I'll land in
verdant fields
in calm water
soothe my soul
immerse me in justice
and truth and
in You

leaning on You
I have no fear
I tread lightly
through valleys
and shadows
and nightmares and terror
of doomsday and
death

Your bounty sustains me
I drink my fill
my thirst is quenched
and I  empowered
by Your master plan
can face whatever
comes my way
and live my days
in peace

# 24

it's all God's
the endless universe
and everything within
belong to Him
God set up oceans patterns
galaxies and DNA

so who of us could ever
reach the top
to rise above ourselves
to keep our hearts and deeds
as pure as God's intent

perhaps it's those
who seek to know His ways
those blessed
in the endeavor
in the quest to find
and open gates of heaven
to see God
the source of all
unknown

# 25

I bring myself to You
trusting
You won't turn away
but will accept me
and show me a path
back to You

Remember mercy
forget the sins of my youth
open a door
to awareness of You
an unveiling to calm my soul
I'm trapped in a maze
with a net at my feet
and You
are my only way out

so turn to me  hear me
be kind and forgive
I'm poor and alone
and pursued
by enemy forces
beyond my control
I reach out to You
still  again

# 26

look inside the me of me
into my eyes into my soul
and see my love
unwavering
my love for You is real
present  if You look or not
there  if You care or not

test me if you doubt my love
golden through fire
it will only emerge
refined
unscorched
rekindled

I play by Your rules
not theirs
it's Your light up ahead
that guides my path

I've washed my hands
of things I've done
and stay away from
dirt

I've found myself
my space that's Yours
Your place Your palace
You
and now in found
tranquility
I pray You
keep me there

# 27

God, with You
lighting my way
shielding me
what could I fear

You've saved me before
I've seen them fall
those who conspire
to devour me
I've seen them
armies of them
weaken and fall
now my heart
has no fear
only desire
for Your ongoing
presence

let me in
to the safety of You
when times get tough
again
open Your gates to me
welcome me
shelter me
nourish me
let me in
I'll get strong and face them
yet again and win again
and let them know
You arm me

I'm orphaned and alone
at war
I need Your arms
I need to trust
to know You're here
lighting my path
giving me hope
and showing me
the way   out

# 28

if You don't hear me
if You don't listen
I might go straight
to hell
so help me resist
the easy slide
into mire
the pull to deceive
temptation to lie
to myself, others

deception comes easily
I see it all over
how power prestige
can turn some men
into demigods on stilts
heedless of downtrodden
underfoot

Payback time
bring them down
and keep them down
stay true to those
who try to live
in truth

redeem Your people
bless Your land
carry us forever

Your truth is what remains
when human power
wanes

# 29

when you feel strong
invincible
give God His due
in your honest
inner life
know your power
stems from Him

Hear His voice
in tranquil seas
in crashing waves

Hear His voice
in stormy winds
as limbs of cedars
leap like unicorns
across the sky
their beauty His
unspeakable

Hear His voice
in fire
in silent desert nights
in cries of babies
in the dark

Hear seraphim
in His chambers
whisper holy holy holy
giving credit
where all credit
must be due

know that as the
flood was His
so will the blessed
peace bequeathed
to us
be His
to give

# 30

I proclaim You most high
You've raised me
from depths unfathomable
lifted me above strife
healed my deadly wounds
carried me out of hell
cleansed my soul
of despair

sing out to God
give thanks and praise
acknowledge Him
remember

things change
in a heartbeat
life flips
in a minute
terror of night
can end with day
security is not secure
Your will controls us all
You are the One
who we must seek
and pray to and beseech
for life and time

bereft of You
we turn to dust
can't breathe
can't think
can't sing

but close to You
with boundless thanks
I'm stepping out of shrouds
embracing life
with holy joy
my dance begins
anew

# 31

when I lean on You
I'm stable
Be my rock
my fortress my shelter
I'll find my way to You
far from the trap I'm in
I'll place my life
in Your hands
and stop relying on
false guards

O the joy the rapture
to know that You're with me
when I'm left for dead
my hope is with You
not with bodyguards
generals armies and spies

Background noises
plots and whispers
shake my faith
in man
at times in haste
when faced with death
I've also doubted
You

but blessed God
my soul is Yours
my time is Yours to give
I'm not ashamed
to say aloud
I trust in You alone

let prideful babbling foolish men
have shame in arrogance
Lord shine on me
and on all souls who love You
in good faith
and give us strength
and courage
to wait for You
and wait

# 32

Lucky is he
who doesn't try
to cover up
misdeed
but openly
admits
repents
comes clean
with God and man

for days and heavy nights
my silent sins
gnawed at the marrow
of my bones
and left me
parched

when I reach out to God
in prayer
regretting deeds I never
should have done
He can be kind to me
forgiving
and bestow
upon me mercy
undeserved

don't be an ass an ox a horse
and stand there mute
bedecked with jewels
while in your heart
deceit grows thick
with unchecked sins

cleanse your hands
your soul your heart
and try to make amends
then call to God
in truth  and pray
you aren't washed away

# 33

Sing out to God
O righteous men
and women
Praise Him now!
with music
with a whole new song
with choirs
orchestras!

Proclaim to all
that God controls
the heavens, oceans
 us
that He is truth
that endlessly
He gives

that we are always
in His hands
His thoughts
His plans
and all we are we see we know
arise from His design

His energy empowers
without bounds
and those of us
who can admit
that power stems from Him
can find some
inner peace

how true that human might
is weak
that there are forces
out of our control

but when we trust
have faith in God
while trying hard
to help ourselves
there's hope
we may

# 34

I will stay aware and thank You
bless You every day
composing prayers
in song and word
so every letter  a to z
will speak of You
I'll tell the world
whoever's listening
that You hear
You hear us all

When young and hungry lions
prowled in anger round my camp
I cried and
You sent angels
to my side
to hold my hand
and lead me surely
out of danger
certain death
and when I called You
I  somehow
emerged intact

My children
open up your hearts
and let these teachings
enter and take root
and if you want to live and
love your life and face the trials
that will come
be careful with the words
you say and write
stay true to truth
seek peace be kind
and when the need is there
cry out for help to God
who will be with you
always listening
always there

# 35

Fight for me
aim your arrows
at those who seek my death
speak to me
tell me You're on my side
tell me You're planning
their doom
send me an angel
to keep them at bay
to drive them away
to turn them
to dust

I never saw it coming
they were part of me
I nurtured them
and now they turn around
and try to eat my flesh

I'm crying out to You
come here come now
don't turn away
attention must be paid
they have the strength of lions
see me as their prey
and want to eat me whole

I'm weak they're hungry
only You can change
the course of any war
restore my hope

so fight for me
let me survive
and I'll write  poems  songs
I'll tell the world
I won't be shy  embarrassed  coy
to say
You save

# 36

when sinning dictates
to my heart of hearts
   be brave and stay the course
   no one is watching
schemes I plan
at night
in bed
come easy
slick

but God in clouded distance
reigns and judges all
shows mercy undeserved
to man
and even
beast
and in this knowledge
I find comfort

I can hide beneath
Your wings
find cover
in the gentle mercy
always there
beneath Your wings
and find there
light
and air to breathe
and water for my soul
to be reclaimed
from prideful
lawless power
easy
O so easy
in my hands

# 37

so you never shine
and they do
so you're poor and give
and they're rich and don't
you struggle
they thrive
in their careless lives
in their wanton easy lives
don't despair don't compare
they'll be mowed down
like grass
in time they will
and you won't

let your answer be silence
when questions of fairness
worm into and gnaw
at your soul
find joy in the good
and delight in the lot
that is yours to inherit and keep
and trust that God knows
who is just who provides
and whose seed will take root
and survive

and He knows who's a meteor
flash in the pan
evanescent and
brilliant then
gone

# 38

dear God
dear  punishing God
Your arrows
hit their mark
and I can't breathe
with shattered bones
can't run

my sins an evil halo
swirl around my head
land on my shoulders
a yoke
too heavy
to bear

I'm crushed
I'm dust
before I'm dead
I'm mute to all
they can't console

I speak to You alone
and limping wounded
and in pain
and fearing fate I must deserve
I pray
Forgive

# 39

I wanted to be mute
accept Your will
keep it in
not complain
not erupt and say
what I never
should have said

Tell me
what's my life to You
my speck of dust
of a life
to You
in Your infinite
inconceivable
spacetime

Hear me
Care for me
I'm a guest of Yours
on earth
and I will
silently
accept the fate
that's mine to bear
that's Yours to give
if You only
let me
be me
in peace
before
I have
to go

# 40

I knew Your will
would be
I hoped Your will
would coincide
with mine
I hoped You'd care
for me

Now here I am
so joyous  high
above the quicksand
that was killing me
and flowing from my lips and pen
are songs of praise
of You
O lucky me
and he or she
who put their trust
in You
and stay away
from charlatans
ubiquitous
and lame

What can I ever
give to You
What could You want
from me
I've learned I'm learning
it's not
human sacrifice

I want to follow You
and make Your will
be my desire
the blood and guts of me
and get it out
and publish  shout
in God I trust

# 41

Happy is he who knows
that bad times pass
that things change fast
that you can rise
from a bed drenched
with hopeless blood and tears
that your heart can pour itself
to God
Who cares

when I heard whispers
in the hall
that death is near
but to my face
came lies
that all is well
when optimistic friends
retreated   disappeared
when I had fewer hairs
than pains
when fog obscured my sight
when my heart lacked strength
to beat again
I begged You
to have mercy
and repair
my wretched body
damaged soul

You stay by me
You never go
You're here
You're real
You heal
and I simply
believe in You
Amen
oh man
Amen

# 42

like a parched doe
near a cool stream
I thirst for the essence
of You
Your water
O my living God
I yearn to know
You

I felt close to You once
I remember the joy
of the presence of You
within me
stability peace
was my daily bread
the holidays Sabbaths
the songs

and now I drink
tears
am bereft
have no clue
cannot fathom
the depth of You

from deep within
I call to the void
in the forest the ocean
the sky
and I search and I wait
as I reach out to You
so desperate
for Your reply

don't cry my soul
just praise my God
He hears me
He'll reply

# 43

You be my judge
side with me
set me free

Why am I captive
in enemy chains
alone in this vise
despised

Come to me
with angels bearing
light and truth
good news
and lift me high above
this blackened night

and then aloft
unchained
I'll fly
and know
that it was You
and You alone
who got me
out

I'll write You songs
of love and praise
and sing
and play them on my harp
and in my head

# 44

We've heard
we've learned from history
from fathers  Torah
past
that You determine
outcome
it's Your will

that we must try
and we can fight
but if we win
all victories
are Yours
without You
all our swords
are blunt

so now
my fathers' God, and mine
command whatever powers that be
to bend to us
our armies can't prevail alone
and if we triumph
as we did
we always will
give thanks to You

when You turn away from us
we're prey  we're lambs
they're wolves
they eat their fill
and scatter our remains

we trust in You
we're killed for this
return to us
dear God return
we never have left
You

# 45

*for the groom*

    the ink flows
    from my soul to my pen
    as I write in praise of you
    brave prince among men
    the words from your mouth
    are faceted brilliant jewels
    you are beautiful  wise
    and blessed to rise
    above the rest of us
    stay strong  stay humble
    vanquish foes
    be fruitful righteous
    grow
    and remain adorned
    and adored for all time
    as you are by your bride
    today

*for his bride*

    virgin beauties flock in droves
    and he desires your love
    it's time to stand
    beside your man
    and leave your childhood
    home
    to take your place
    and walk with him
    on paths unknown
    as queen
    he sees you precious sparkling
    and bejeweled
    he knows your soul
    and needs you  wants you
    for his own  alone
    be good to him
    and make his palace
    home
    and live with him and progeny
    forever blessed
    within

# 46

in the worst of times
it's easiest to find You

when earth and life
turn upside down
foundations quake
and mountains lose control
we're not afraid
we need You
and You're there with us
in silence
through the crash

and though our planet's
rearranged
we focus and we see
the great can fall
the weak can rise
and tranquil rivers
from above
can calm the raging madness
and put out
the fires of war

# 47

Gather everyone
Applaud!
Sing praise!
Ring bells!
Rejoice!

Blast the shofars
trumpets horns
Proclaim that God is King
and we're His love

He's King
He's chosen us
to watch
to know
that He's in charge
and that He has
the power
to protect

His Kingdom
everything
conceivable
and not

# 48

God's power
immense
is there
you can see it
in holy Jerusalem
home
in beautiful earth
in mountains
and landscapes
His universe
palaces
fit for
the King

the rulers here
of flesh and blood
all labor and beget
more trembling
mortal flesh
and blood
a breeze a breath
a thought
from God
can crash their ships
against the rocks
or make them
blow away

we hope
imagine
that You will
be true to us
and kind and just
and like the hills
around the mount
of Zion and Jerusalem
You will protect
and cradle us
to the end
of worlds
and time

# 49

Listen to this
rich man poor man
cave dwellers all
of unstable earth
Listen to the music
of the wisdom
of my heart
and know my song
is true
and know that I don't
live in fear
of death
as some
mortals
do

there's no first class
round trip to the grave
and you can't be
ransomed out
and all of your
power and wealth and fame
count as much in the end
as a pasture does
to a slaughtered
calf

What matters most
what lives beyond
the other side of life
is not of matter
not our bodies
bound for mother earth
and not the moneyed towers
we have built
but deeds we've done
and kindnesses
each one immortal
measured cherished counted
loved  by God

# 50

Great God Speaks
perfection
rises over Zion in the east
and bathes the earth
in beauty and light

thundering judgment
reigns beneath
the brightened sky
and all is known

> *keep your bloody sacrifices*
> *sacred cows and flesh*
> *don't offer Me*
> *what's Mine in any case*
> *you've no control*
> *where matter is concerned*
>
> *come seek Me with*
> *what's in your realm*
> *your soul*
> *your power to choose*
>
> *approach Me*
> *shed deceit*
> *be real*
> *come clean*
>
> *and stand exposed*
> *in My pure light*
> *with every truth*
> *revealed*

# 51

Show clemency to me
dear God
I've sinned
I see sins in my mirror
filthy potent in my gut
royal
mortal
sins

I'm broken now
in pieces
on the ground
and only You
who formed me
in my mother's womb
know human weakness
is a part
of man
so look away
from what I've done
and take me
as I am
repentant
working on my soul
and get me out of this
alive and clean
and bring me back
the holy joy
of being whole
with You
so I can teach
all sinners
that the sacrifice
You won't reject
is a humbled heart
still true to You
still yearning
to come home

# 52

Don't pride yourself
on all your wealth
your mouth's your only strength
with its tongue that
thinks and speaks and acts
a sharpened razor
broken glass
feeding on lies
and dealing death
and spouting slander out

You're high on words
but God will bring you
down and break
your wicked tongue
and shatter it
and silence you for good
and wise men seeing this
will nod their heads
and point you out
and know that you're an evil fool
immersed in stealth  deceit
and self

I trust in God
live in His house
I'm evergreen
renewed
my olive branches spanning worlds
remain abundant
blessed strong
survive and thrive
by God

# 53

in silence the villain
says to himself
there is no god
no one is good
I'm not alone
we're all depraved
look at the chosen ones
united in their choice
of sin
conspiring and corrupt
oblivious
to a creator
no one knows
the things
we do

but God
unknowable
keeps track
keeps faith
and listens listens
for a human cry
so that
He can
respond

so call to Him
and may He hear
and send salvation
starting now
from Zion
radiating
to encompass
all of man
and freeing us
from dangers
at our borders
and from demons
deep within

# 54

I'm calling You by name
almighty God
I beg of You
to hear me
listen closely
if no sound comes out
I pray you
read my lips

the strangers
who are after me
don't know that You
are there for me
to foil their
evil plans

and when You do
I will give thanks
to You
with every
sacrificial
breath
that I
have left

I will
outlast
my foes
but keep
them all
in sight

# 55

I'm burdened trembling
terrified
and begging of You
not to hide from me
in distant Godly skies
while I'm surrounded
on the ground
by accusations
evil shrieking voices
flinging hatred at me
fast

if only I could rise
above it all
sprout wings
and be alone
with You
in quiet
sheltered
peace

the treachery within my walls
untethered me
and now I doubt
that I can trust
my bosom friends
whose words were
sweet and wise
and soft
convincing
cursed
lies

I'm shedding
sandbags of deceit
for You to judge
they're in Your hands
I'm letting go
to fly

# 56

O God have mercy
every day
I run away
from hostile hordes
all chasing me
relentlessly
they congregate
and spy on me
and count my steps
and wait

they've caught me now
I'm in a vise
as they compete
for the prize
of my head

I crouch in caves
cry hurricanes
and trust that You
collect each solitary tear
to cleanse
and polish my poor soul

what have I to fear of man
when I still stand
and still can pray
to God
who keeps
my burnished soul
protected
in His light

# 57

Lord have mercy
take me in
so that the cooling shadows
of Your wings
protect me
and relieve the heat
until this fury passes
and I'm safe

cage the lions
prowling round my cave
tongues and arrows
saber teeth and swords
unite in desire
for my life
as nets of fire
hem me in

awaken, soul
and shake off panic
stifled hope
get up and pray
and sing out loud
take out your harp
and rouse the dawn
and beg the Lord of heavens
to make light
of night
to day

# 58

How can you be silent
not declare me
innocent
when you have
the power
to help

you must know
right from wrong
but your muted tongue
has a will of its own
and your hands
steeped in blood
have no heart

like a snake
uncharmed
by his master's flute
you remain immobile
deaf
you've earned
and deserve
the silence
of death

God break the wicked
long before their baby teeth
turn into fangs
make them retreat
turn into snails
curl into shells
and make their wombs
their tombs

then the oppressed
will know of God
that justice reigns
that virtue can bear fruit

# 59

throw me a rope
a straw to grasp
and lift me up and out of here
show me a light
to focus on
as I sit here trapped
and they come in stealth
amassing on the fragile
membrane of my cell

they drool like dogs
and bark their lies
incriminating me
denying You
they circle round
and round
noses to the ground
sniffing for hope
to destroy

redeem your loyal subjects
let the evil rabid dogs
all die like dogs

I raise my sights to heaven
knowing I'm within Your reach
You can find me in a crater
rescue me from any pit
if I just sing to You
You'll hear me
in Your tower
high  away

# 60

Is this a test
did I not do what's right
that now I have to fight
bewildered as a drunk
unclear of why
we were attacked
and here we are again at war
without a better reason than
we
didn't
start
it

we fight and kill
on shaky ground
not knowing
where it all
will end

remember each of us
by name
remember Judah and Menashe
and Ephraim and Gilad
husbands fathers brothers
all beloved sons
and bring us home again
to wives
and
daughters

# 61

Hear O Lord
as David sings
a prayer to You

From the ends of the earth
I call to You
You take my hand
and lead me to
Your tower fortress
walls of rock
protecting me
no enemy
can reach me now
I want to stay
and hide here
for all time
but I have promises to keep
and miles to go
before I sleep

so give me strength
and give me time
so I can pay my dues
and try to meet
whatever comes
live out my days
with hope sustained
by closeness God
to You

# 62

Only God
> knows my silent self
> true to Him
> true to me

Only God
> is my source of hope
> my anchor
> when at sea

why would I lean
on a broken fence
when God is a fortress
and strength and reserve
come from Him

Only man
> delusional
> puts faith
> in power
> money
> air

Only man
> a puff of smoke
> can live a shameless lie
> and call it true

Only God
> when judging man
> determines
> what he's due

# 63

My tired body rises
as the sun begins to parch another day
and O my God
I thirst for You

I search for You
through searing light
and dream of knowing You
in holiness
the vision of it
precious
as my life

You're not mirage
You are oasis
always there
I long to cling to You
and drink of You
and sing to You
replenished
never leave
and my reward in reaching You
will far surpass
the sweetest waters
I could find

I know that when I'm on my watch
beneath the stars
deep in the cooling desert nights
I'm not alone
I am at one with You
and those who seek my harm
are doomed to fall
and fail
again

# 64

it may look as though
I'm mumbling to myself
but I am calling You
so hear me
I am praying
for my life

my foes collaborate
conspire against me
search my files to look for dirt
bury landmines in my path
sharpen teeth and knives and razors
aim to kill

they don't know me
don't know You
don't admit
that in an instant
You can twist
their tongues and guns
their pens and arrows
change the course of war

when You do
all those who can
will see Your hand
in victory
rejoicing
grateful
ever grateful
that You haven't
looked away

# 65

Wait for us
though silent now
we'll come to you in Zion
singing praise

Keep the heavens open
drench our land
with mist and dew
and when the bounty comes
we'll know it comes
from You

Flocks of sheep
white as clouds
obscure our verdant hills
newborn babies pink and healthy
come with ease into our lives
our fields are ripe and sweet
with fat of land
and salt of earth

Sated
we'll remember You
keep our word
bring You joyous tithes
and tell ourselves we're giving back
but know
that what You really want of us
is just
to search for You
ascend to You

# 66

Voices from all corners of the earth
sing out in harmony
a symphony of awe and praise
to honor the Creator
of us all

Acknowledge that He rules
and seek Him
in the oceans He has moved
to let your feet
walk on dry land
see Him
in the molecules of water
in the channels
of your cells
find Him in the infinite
infinitesimal

Enter His domain
keep promises you made
when in distress
see Him in the soul of man
the eyes of sacrificial cows
the wings of butterflies
and tails of comets

Search for Him revere Him
even when you may be forced
to walk through fire
and if you somehow manage
to emerge alive  intact
as I have done
know
that when you're blessed
it's by the grace
of God

# 67

keep the blessings coming
rain  predictable and gentle
sun  to warm our fields and pastures
 and our homes
light our paths
our lives
our seasons
notice everyman
and everyone
will know Your name
and thank You
as we toil  and sow  and reap
and we harvest
cornucopias
of plenty

# 68

When God's presence is revealed
and truth prevails
corrupt foundations crack
mountains fall
earthquakes melt golden calves
and righteous men see God's design
in this reordering of power
and rejoice

unrepentant self-made masters
run for cover in the flattened plains
the landscape's changed
to nourish those returning
day by day
each blessed day a gift
as wayward sons
come home
assume their rightful places
under God
bulls and bears and
students housewives
Jew and gentile
visionaries
workers rulers
princes kings
all congregate to sing
Your praise

# 69

Help me God before I drown
the water's rising to my neck
and I can't breathe or move
I'm trapped in quicksand
enemies metastasizing everywhere
exact their toll
and I have nothing left
to give
Is there a better time than now
for You to hear me cry

don't let those who need You
lose all hope because they think
that You have left me here
to die
You who know me
You who see me broken
You who have forgiven
my past sins

turn Your tide against my foes
Bleed them  blot them
from Your book of life
Wipe them out
count their sins

make me an example of Your mercy
and I'll sing so all of earth and heaven hear
that fearing  serving  loving  God
redeems

# 70

Quickly come to me
my God
and take my side

Shame on them
pity them
stigmatizing me
for curses that befell me
who knows why
they lack pity and compassion
cluck their tongues
as I am shunned
while they secretly are glad
to see me fall

Turn Your back on them
and stand by me
hasten my recovery
restore the life that I have known
so all of us who can
will see
that those in need
who seek Your help
will get Your help
and recognize Your greatness
and rejoice in You
and me

# 71

I still rely on You my God
to keep protecting me

When I was a child
I trusted You
I spoke to You
You answered me
and now I'm old
and weak and needy
don't abandon me

the sharks smell blood
and circle for the kill
emboldened
sensing I'm alone

but You who are eternal
steadfast faithful righteous great
are with me always
never leave me
I still look to You for aid
and though You've tested me
and test me yet again
I cannot help but reach for You
and sing to You and praise You
You are mine
and You are there for me
in old age
as in youth

# 72

Judge me
God of Israel
but please my Lord
be charitable with my son
my heir
my Solomon

Let his reign
be like the rain
that falls on orchards
sees them blossom
and bear fruit

Make him notice the oppressed
as well as those more blessed
and let his rulings be
compassionate and just

Have kings of other nations
look to him
to emulate and adulate
bathe his life in golden light
and bless his name eternally
his name my name
my prayer
Amen

# 73

Better men than I
know God is good
but I for one
have had my doubts

I've seen how evildoers
flourish and succeed
I've envied them
their lives of ease
longevity and health
and their cocksuredness
in self
I've heard them speak from lofty places
spewing dirt
negating You
and wondered why I always try
to keep my thoughts and speech and deeds
in check  in purity for You
when I am plagued all day all night
with my troubled tortured life
and You don't care

I am anguished  mortal  clueless
but I somehow sense You
everywhere
and know that You and only You
retain the power
to flip a life
so those on tops of mountains
slip and
in an instant fall
from grace
but I have seen You
just as quickly
lift the righteous to the skies
on angel wings

I trust that You will guide me
hold my hand and not let go
stay by my side be close to me
and hear me pray and speak to You
and know I lean
on You alone

# 74

Don't forget that
You chose us
long ago  in better times
when we were young
You carried us into Your home
made us aware of You
Remember us

With passing time
we've come to see our temple crash
as enemies build idols
in our holy inner spaces
and we know
that they're Your adversaries too

They're burning generations
of Your people
of Your teachings
and their axes
plunder forests of Your trees
we're banished from the homes we built
according to Your plans

We're slaves of man
of lawless beasts
but trust in You
to end this reign
to lift us gently up and out
to handle us with care
and lovingly dispatch us
to the skies You have created
and like homing pigeons
we'll return to You

# 75

We who try
to know You
reach You
pray You
don't destroy us
in our search
for the sublime

> *your world is fluid*
> *My design*
> *and I will choose*
> *the place and time*
> *to rearrange*
> *the order*
> *up or down*

Stop the haughty sinners
planting flags
in their secure positions
in the desert on the mountains
claiming turf

Show them
You make victors
You decide
who wears the crown
who drinks the wine
and who will sip
the bitter dregs

# 76

God is known in Judah
and Jerusalem
His name revered in Zion
where He's fought

and though we know
He's everywhere
it's easier to find Him
where He's sought

God of Israel
Source of power
confound plans
to harm Your land
pulverize the weapons
aimed at us
before
they explode
in our homes

Send amoral armies running
scared and scattered
flying backwards
impotent and blind
make their kings
and dictators
stand humbly
as defendants
in Your court
bring them down
to final justice
waiting deep within the earth

# 77

when I can't speak
but my voice just cries
and cries to You
in pain
when I can't sleep
and my arms are powerless
but reach for You
in vain
when I can't think
but my soul still yearns for You
with doubt

do You hear me
as I thought You did
do You collect my tears
or do they fall into a void
have You abandoned me

when this fear
evokes more terror
than my wounds
I remind my pounding heart
that You are there
I must have faith
I cannot understand
Your plan
but know You can
and will deliver
turn the tide
and send a Moses or an Aaron
lead me to a better place
a milk and honey
promised land

# 78

Pay attention
to the truth
read white spaces
between lines
and teach your children
ancient Torah
that you know
or think you know
search for threads
that unify
the tapestry of history
so progeny may bow
to God's design

tell of forefathers
who strayed  rejected God
or maybe just forgot
His presence in their lives
tell of wonders supernatural
plagues on Egypt
walls of water standing tall protecting us
and crashing on the heads of Pharaoh's men
tell of manna from the sky
water spouting in the desert
from a rock

tell of those
who reached for God
when they felt
the need for God
but scorned Him
when they didn't need His help

God turned from those
who turned from Him
and chose instead
the seed of David
loyal shepherd poet king
to carry His inheritance
with pride and love and deed

# 79

my God
they've broken into
holy spaces
spreading filth

our corpses lie exposed
and birds are pecking
at our flesh

blood flows freely
in the streets
nations cross the line
to gawk and mock
denying that You care

we've sinned
we know
but how much longer
will You punish us
Unleash Your wrath
on people who deserve it
more

let us heal
have mercy God
avenge us sevenfold
we'll follow You
like sheep
we'll always follow You
and fear and love You
seek You
praise You
Lord

# 80

Shepherd of Israel
You know love
show Yourself
You who dwell
between the cherubs
You who knew
of Jacob's love
his Rachel love
the children of that love
by name
the Yosef and Menashe
Binyamin Ephraim love

You who can uproot with love
You who took us out of Egypt
brought us home
to nurture us
until we covered Israel
with our vines

keep the hungry boars away
the ones who chew our roots
and trample shoots
come back to Your vineyard
and tend to us
with love again
with clouds of dew
and sun again
and watch us thrive

# 81

Sing to God
in joy and strength
with harps and violins
with trumpets shofars
saxophones and drums
mark time keep track
of each new moon
and celebrate another chance
another month to live and grow
as Joseph did on foreign soil
knowing God was with him
pit to prison
houseboy
to viceroy

listen closely
try to hear
the song of God
and follow it
though you are deaf
and it is dark
and you are blinded
by your quest for things
that fade

God's music plays for you
and if you seek it
it is there
and if you heed it
it is sweet
and can fulfill
beyond desire

# 82

In God we trust
to stand for justice
in the courts of man and God
but here on earth
the weak are sentenced
those with power
get off

stretch to reach
the drowning
overwhelmed
unfairly judged
the homeless
and the helpless
and the poor
the all alone
who walk in darkness
with no hope
of ever seeing
light

In you they trust
though you be mortal
judge or general or king
be godlike fair to all
and pray
that when you die
as they will
you'll find mercy
in the court

# 83

now is not the time
dear God
for silence or withdrawal
our ancient foes
the Philistines
and sons of Ishmael
from Edom Moav Amalek
Assyria and Tyre
have terrorized Your world
as they collaborate
with modern hate
to stream and form
a river
rushing toward us
in jihad
poison
to obliterate
us all

now's the time
right now's the time
for You to show
that power is Yours
that if You will
a glance a puff
can blow them all away
like straw in wind
like straw in fire
like dung
that returns
to the earth

let them learn
to see the shame
of murder suicide and war
and let them see
You reign
in peace

# 84

How sweet it could be
to call Your place
my home
to live where You dwell
to know that
my eggs are safe
in Your nest
to have the keys
to get inside
behind Your walls

how lucky are they
who find the strength
to follow You
and praise Your path
even as they walk
through tears
they drink
from springs
of faith

a single day of life
with hope
is better than thousands
without
better than decades
of doubt

please hear me God
and let me in
I know You're home

happy are they
who trust You

# 85

You wanted us home
in Your land
You brought us back
forgave us
gathered our sins
and Your wrath
and buried them both
that was then
and this is now
we've strayed
and need mercy
again

dwell within us
where we live
let truth and kindness merge
let peace and justice intermingle
and take root in fertile earth
and rain on us
from heaven
gently

step by step
we will return
to be with You
in the place
we know
is home

# 86

Listen to me
I am needy and bereft
I trust You
to show mercy

all day long
I cry to You
beseeching You
to hear my prayers
to lift my soul
to bring me joy
again
I call to You
when I'm in pain
because I know
You'll answer

nothing can compare
to You Your deeds Your miracles
unify my heart's desires
to seek Your truth
to shed false skin
and still remain protected
to honor You and thank You
for redeeming me
from godless foes
who sought my soul

Look at me
be gracious to me
give me strength to carry on
send me a sign
that You still care
that You're still there
beside me

# 87

when holiness
is the foundation
bedrock of a soul
or city
Godliness can enter
through the gates

fortunate are those
conceived within

each one precious
from the start
each one counted
and protected
each one nurtured
from the womb
with thoughts
of God

each one special
as is Zion
to the Jews

# 88

I cried by day
at night
I stood in prayer
my God Almighty
save me

I've had my fill
of trouble
I am ready
for the grave
I'm numb
I've lost all strength
to cope

You've shown me
only wrath
You have abandoned me
I have no friends
You've lowered me
into a pit
I am half dead

every day begins
with prayer
my arms reach up
to You
I hope for miracles
though You are far
and I am suffocating
all alone
and in the dark

# 89

I sing of the loving
kindness
on which Your world
is built
the heavenly order
that rules

I sing of the promises
You made
to build the house of David
and nourish his seed
for all time

I sing of the oneness
of Adonai
Creator of the sea
and stars and earth
and sky and all
of us

I sing of Your throne
eternal
erected in mercy and truth

lucky are nations
who follow You
Your prophets knew
that David's house
is one that would
and they entreated him
to base his earthly throne
on lovingkindness
too

in time, in turn
as David's children
stay with You
or stray from You
we still are
intertwined with You
remember and
be kind

# 90

Our ancestors and progeny
all dwell within
the endless time and space
You made
from nothing

mornings noons
and decades
stream by us
relentlessly

You have given
us the power to change
regret the past
and keep our eyes
on present deeds
as we return to You

buds at sunrise
blooms at noon
withered chaff by night
we race through time
and waste our fleeting years

You push us
to the brink
then say
Return
when will You
return to us
sate us with as much
delight
as You have
with sorrow

teach us how
to live our lives
to build immortal souls
with deeds of splendor
that will meet Your expectations of us
lofty though they be

# 91

He sits hidden somewhere
in shadows of ineffable secrecy
and I tell Him
You are my refuge
my protector
I trust You
keep me safe

He will cover you
He'll shield you
take you under His wing
take a bullet for you
or an arrow
or whatever whizzes past your head
endangering your life
your soul  your loves
Lift your eyes
and see the wicked
fall in droves
while you remain intact
He will order angels
to guard you and yours
everywhere
to carry you
when the land gets rough
you'll crush the heads
of snakes and lions
evil will never
befall your house

He knows my name
He knows I'm His
He answers me

> *I am your refuge*
> *your protector*
> *I will be with you*
> *through hard times*
> *you will live*
> *a long good life*

# 92

it's good to pause
to praise the Lord
and notice all you have
with Sabbath eyes

to take the sofa
off your back
and sit

to start the morning
sing the dawn
and see the work of God

to slow
the pace
of time

to wonder at the colors
and the fragrance of the earth
to look up and
to see cerulean skies

to wait until the stars bring back
inevitable night
and you resume your search
to gather shards
of shattered light

those who never stop
to lift their eyes
can't contemplate
the work
of God

the righteous are renewed by God
like palm trees near a stream
like cedars old and strong
and evergreen

# 93

God rules
behind the scenes
cloaked in grandeur
and power
and the majesty
of nature

oceans and motion
follow His laws
galaxies
obey
strings of cosmos
heed His word

ever loyal
all bear witness
to eternal
holy
truths

# 94

God of vengeance God of right
reveal Yourself
and show all those
abusing might
that You give back
what they deserve

nazis cossacks haman satan
terrors of the night
how much longer
will they have
the upper hand
confident
as they devour innocents
at will
randomly destructive
they declare that You don't care

do they not know
that He who made the ear
can hear
that He who formed the eye
can see
that You have access
to their inner thoughts
and know them
to the core

that You're the holy spark of hope
that glows within our breast
that You're the rock we cling to
when endangered and oppressed
that we know You
reverse the course of evil
when You wish

send it somersaulting backward
into infinite oblivion
the nothingness
it's due

# 95

Let's call to God
when we're joyful
when times are good
and we're singing

Let's sing to God
express our thanks
acknowledge that
we are aware
that He created
oceans mountains
joy and song
and the mystery
of us

Let's try to accept
His dominance
our need to follow Him
and never again
incur His wrath
as we wander for years
on a desert path
of anger and angst
in a futile search
for a golden calf
that can never
lead us
home

# 96

Sing to God
a different song
a new and ancient
joyous song
Sing like the earth
sing like the whales
so all who try to listen
hear
One God created all

Broadcast news
that God is here
exhort the world
to leave their fragile idols
demigods and lords
One God created all

there's majesty within His court
His gardens all bear gifts
wheat and willow bow to Him
as mountains reaffirm
His righteous reign

Sing out ring bells
of thanks and joy
to God alone
omnipotent
all knowing God
eternal God
the God
who rules
us all

# 97

God is King
so earth be glad

myriad islands
in turquoise and green
sparkle in sunlight
and moonlight

God is King
surrounded by clouds
shrouded
in layers
of gray

God is King
His crystal throne
is clear and etched
in precious stone
each facet
glowing truth

iceberg myths
and mountains melt
as idols crash
and burn in the fire
of His gaze

the righteous
sowing seeds of light
dispel the fog

Happy are they
who do no harm
believers
in God
the promise of life
the mercy of
rainbows

# 98

Another song
a new one now
of miracles
of outstretched arms
that reach for us
and lift us up
with holy strength
unveiled   so doubters
clearly see
the hand of God

Blast the shofars
trumpets horns
come mountains
blow your tops
and roar
as rapid rivers
crash and clap
together sing
with all of life
before the King
who comes to us
a righteous judge
His path to us
and ours to Him
forever
unobstructed

# 99

God is King
He chose us
and we chose Him
and God only knows
which came first

Someday everyone
will choose
and tremble
in awareness of
accountability
to Him

we won't be
the only ones
who see the
inconceivable
cherubic mighty purity
inherent
in His rule

we've been taught
to seek Him
when on mountains
or in valleys
and to find Him
where we are

prophets priests of Israel
Moses Aaron Samuel
called to God
with human angst
and listened
through a fog
to hear His answers
guide their lives

one day  everyone
will meet the Maker
hear His voice
exalt His greatness
bow to Him
alone

# 100

Don't just think it

Speak your mind
and give God thanks
out loud

Sing His praises
serve Him
work with joy

Know that He
created us
that we belong to Him

Come with me now
to bless His name
He has been good to us

Let us trust
that He'll continue
to show kindness
to our children
generations of them
always
in good faith

# 101

this is a song
from me to You
reminding me
that if I want
to be near You
I must act wisely
and be kind

When will You
come to me

I will stay pure
in my thoughts
and heart
in my home
and when
I'm out

I won't eye evil
won't seek trash
and neither
will ever
cling to me

I'll purge my life
of influence
from cheats and sneaks
and liars
steeped in pride

I'll keep my vision
high
surround myself
with upright men
to talk to me
and walk with me
on paths
that lead
to You

# 102

Don't make (me) believe
that You don't see me
in my time of need

See me  hear me
answer me
my time is running out
the sand is racing through the hourglass
I'm withering
I live on ashes air and tears
You have abandoned me

bird on a wire
I stand alone
with a heavy wing
and a broken voice
that cannot sing

I've fallen from my aerie
lie in shadows on the ground
but You are King
of land and sky
Your time is not
my time
Your thoughts are not
my thoughts
and You will see me
from Your holy perch
one day
when Your compassion
reigns

the day has come
for You to rise
expose Your lovingkindness
to the steadfast

Show me mercy
as I need You
now

# 103

Soul of mine
bless my God
and all He does
remember that you're His
that you'll return to Him

bless Him
for healing
for giving
for distancing us
from our misdeeds
and gifting us
second chances
lives we haven't earned
or even dreamed of

bless Him
for serendipity
for all that we savor
for sightings of eagles
soaring high

bless Him
for teaching us
not to despair
we're human
we err
but we can repair our souls
and He divine
with eternal patience
will wait for us

# 104

soul of mine
bless my God
Creator  boundless
veiled in light
draped with cosmic power

You sail clouds across the sky
make messengers of wind and fire
place ground beneath our feet
surround the earth with atmosphere
suspend it in thin air

You determine boundaries
of every niche unique
goats on a mountaintop
rabbits in a hole
lions on the prowl for prey
streams quench thirst
of cedars and birds
as the moon marks time
and the sun knows when
to set

newborn babies breathe new souls
man makes bread out of the soil
and savors its wine and oil

O the joy when You provide
the terror when You don't

I'll sing to You while there's breath in me
and bless You as I live
aware of You  away from sin
Amen
Halleluya

# 105

Thank God in public
write Him songs
and praise His miracles
seek Him find Him
everywhere
so those in search of meaning
notice patterns
that appear

look at nations over time
some will ascend
survive the climb
some won't
look at sons of Israel
humble roots transplanted
onto foreign soil
in hostile lands
again again
and though like Joseph
they can thrive
diaspora is never home
and transplants
often wither

plagues of war and darkness
come with blood and lice
and freezing rain
and death of sons
yet slaves emerged
miraculously free
sheltered by a cloud each day
guided by fire at night
then carried home
on eagle wings
to flower
in the eastern sun

Thank God
Praise one and only God
who gifted land and law to us
eternal homes of Israel

# 106

Halleluya
worlds exist by the mercy of
a God we can't conceive of
and those who can suspend the need
to try to understand Him
may live with faith
and sing His praise
happy are they who do

Remember me God
when You dole out joy
so I can be among the blessed
who get to see
that promises You've made
are kept

forget my father's sins and mine
forget the wrongs we've done
negating You as You nourished us
forget that You've seen us
rebellious entitled
cavorting with idols
and steeped in innocent blood
Remember when Moses
our leader  defender beseeched You
have mercy  forgive
*Adonai Adonai El rachum vechanun*
*erech apayim rav chesed emet*
Remember You listened
forgave
How far we've strayed
to live in worlds
from which You have
withdrawn

we're ready to
return to You
so gather our remnants
and bring us home
and we'll know You again
and bless You  Amen
forever
Halleluya

# 107

you who have passed through narrow straits
and emerged  so far  intact
thank God who is good and merciful
thank God who brings you back

you who have wandered in deserts
cloaked in hunger and thirst
crying to God from the depths of despair
then finding a way back home
thank God who is real
works miracles
remember to give back
with your hands and your hope
and your story to tell

you who have known
the razor of loss
and have been left
bereft
abandoned in hospitals nursing homes jails
marking the days toward death
thank God who is good and merciful
thank God who brings you back

you who have lived to
breathe free air
see iron curtains fall
thank God who is One all powerful
thank God who breaks down walls

you who've survived tornadoes
earthquakes tsunamis and war
you who have seen the hand of God
reverse the acid tide
to sweeten springs
and moisten sands
allowing fruit to grow

praise God who ennobles the humbled
bless God who is seen by the wise

# 108

In glory days
and when in need
my heart is loyal
up at dawn
to sing to You
with harp and strings
a reveille of praise

Arise O nations
congresses and parliaments
to sounds of truth
and hear the music
in the sky
and wake up strong and sure
you are a guest
in God's domain

reach for me God
and hear my psalms
and guide me always
shape my will
to bend to Yours
and keep me able
to sustain
my life  my land  my people

teach me how
to give and take
while knowing
all is Yours

# 109

my God   my own exalted God
Do not be silent now
evil spits its filthy lies
and bloody libel
everywhere
it fills the air with poison smoke
that saturates the atmosphere
and chokes the breath of innocents
rewarding trust
with murder

Here on earth now
evil reigns
merciless amoral wicked
crouching at membranes and portals and doors
ready to pounce
and blot out life
and suffocate all prayer
sometimes it wears a human mask
sometimes it hovers in ether or gas

Obliterate eradicate
its name its progeny
Send angels of death
to slaughter its mother
purge its every seed
Be merciless
so there will be no trace of it
no memory  no scent
Send Satan himself
to finish the job

and let the humble and oppressed
arise though wounded
stumbling hungry
ravaged hollow dazed
Help them recover so all will see
their bones come alive
the work of Your hands
a phoenix renewed

so help me God  exalted God
we will rejoice  again

# 110

God said to you
> *sit on my right*
> *stay close*
> *and wait*

He told you
He would fight for you
place your foes
on their knees
at your feet

that though young
you would rule
in their midst
unafraid

that your people would rally
emerge with the dawn
glistening with dew
bearing gifts for you

He gave you His word
He would never regret
crowning you His
eternally

He chooses who
will reign on earth
which heads will roll
whose tongue will taste
the dust of death
which king will drink
sweet water

# 111

Halleluya
I will thank God
in my heart of hearts
as I sit among scholars in intimate rooms
as I speak aloud before crowds

His deeds are great
His energy unspeakable
and formidable
giving  healing
infinite and just
kind and loving
merciful to us

His name is holy
He is One
we cannot comprehend
but we can pray and question
and have faith
and those who fear Him
only Him
rejoice to see
their terrors lose power
their beasts in shreds

Until the end of time and worlds
trials will come from God
to burnish life  revealing
what is shining what is real
to help us shed the empty shells
that crumble to dust
when touched

knowledge stems from
the fear of God
and human vulnerability
wise men know
that the unknown x
we yearn to solve
is zero
we are nothing
but for God

# 112

Happy is he
who's afraid of God
and desperately wants
to please Him
by living a life
based on good deeds
and generosity

Seeds of kindness
sown by him
fall everywhere
on fertile soil
and thrive eternally
he has no need
to fear ill winds
bad news  the dark
his path is clear
his heart is light
he's loved
and revered
by the family
of man

those who choose
a selfish life
grasping hoarding
helping none
gnash their teeth
at the end of the day
full of just
regrets

# 113

Halleluya
think of God
with gratitude
notice those
who serve Him in good faith
emulate the fortunate
who see Him
feel His presence
in the hours
and the minutes
of their lives

greater than
an earthly reign
His kingdom spans
the heavens

who but He
could ever be
in charge of life
and notice me
down here

redeeming me
from poverty
and garbage and filth
to sit among princes
rulers of men
replacing my barrenness
aimlessness  hell
with fertile
productive
joy

# 114

When Israel escaped from Egypt
sons of Jacob fleeing flying
cruelty pursuing
in dead heat
they made it home
to Israel
a holy land
as sovereign people
bowing to God's rule

the raging sea
became a path
to shelter them
and guide them out

the rivers ran upstream
and rocky mountains
leapt like rams
to heed the will
of God

what is real what's miracle
did nature change its course
did mountains leap
did rivers run amok

the Lord of all
creates His laws
and has the power
to bend His laws

to melt a rockhard
cancer mass
converting it
to water

# 115

When You show the watching world
that You are true and kind to us
it's Your name that is glorified
not ours

Why should nations
look at Jews
and wonder if our God
is powerless
or worse
that He has chosen us
to suffer

You are One
the only God
omnipotent and omnipresent
always in our lives

their gods are manmade mindless idols
speechless dumb with silver tongues
golden eyes that lack all vision
ears immune to human cries
hearts of ice and legs of stone
incapable of change
those who put their faith in matter
share its fragile fate

we the house of Aharon
beseech You
love us back
bless us all
with health with life
be good to us
and to our children
and our aged
we are Yours
and want to please You
with our deeds

we can accomplish nothing
from the grave

# 116

I love that God
will hear my voice
and know my racing heart
when I find myself
surrounded by death
and maws of waiting graves

God has mercy
on the simple
and the simply helpless
Hell pursued me
roped me in
its tentacles a noose around my neck
and here I walk
untethered free alive

I knew throughout
You had the power
to mercifully
rescue me

how should I
give back to You
knowing You can
partner with man
precious to You
in life and death

shall I raise a glass and toast You
shall I sacrifice a lamb
shall I orchestrate a gala
in Jerusalem
or shall I try to emulate
Your lovingkindness here
and work with You and serve You
with my deeds

# 117

no matter what
the state of your faith
praise the Maker
of your life

be grateful
be awed
by the truth
of God

# 118

Give thanks to God
the source of good
His mercy sustains all worlds
Come holy man and common man
God-fearing man and frightened man
Admit within and say aloud
His mercy envelops worlds

I pray confined
to a small dark place
where all I see
is a wall in my face
He answers me from
expanses of light
enabling me to see
He's on my right He's by my side
what have I to fear from man
I trust in God and forge ahead
with reason to be brave
I don't have to wait for noble souls
to notice that I am in need
Armies chase me closing in like swarms of bees
and I'm the one who stings with fire
and comes out singing  Halleluya
Listen to the joy the music
coming from a place of faith

Open gates of righteousness
Let me in to walk your paths
These are the gates I want to enter
This is the road I want to take
This is the way I want to thank You
for the gift of life
Here is a block I stumbled on
now stabilizing me
Miraculous reversals
came to be

This is the day God made for us
to celebrate and play
Welcome enter eat with us
and thank the Host who nurtures us
His mercy sustains all worlds

# 119

First comes honesty with self
pure devotion to the truth
then searching for a way to live
and yearning learning how to live
and following Your way to live
then joy

Your words delight my soul
I love to think of You
and speak of You
Unveil my eyes and let me see
Your deeds Your miracles
Your Torah
is my song my hope
my consolation and my crown

How can a man stay whole stay pure
in thought and speech and deed
Teach me how to live my God
Protect me from all fallacy
I yearn for peace my soul is dry
I need You  water me
I am a stranger here on earth
I trust You  stay with me

I have been robbed pursued and slandered
tested and maligned
and all my trials just made me stretch
to reach for You
renewed determined
steadfast in my love
You know me You created me
Do not abandon me
I follow the eternal code
You gave to us for life
I rise at midnight and compose
these psalms for You
I love Your law
and want to live out all my days
immersed in truth
and love of You and feel Your presence
close to me as I stay
close to You

# 120

when I was down
I cried to You
You answered me
I need You now
again

this time to keep me
whole despite
the firestorm
consuming me

tongues of arson
taste my soul
set fire to
undying coals
that burn and burn
within

if only I
had stayed away
alone
a nomad
far from here

I've lived too long
immersed in stealth

I yearn for peace
but when I speak
they answer me
with war

# 121

I lift my eyes
to mountains  skies
and wonder where
relief resides
I know that God
made mountains  skies
and my belief in Him
abides

my God
the Guard of Israel
will never sleep
won't let me fall
He watches me
protects me from
the midnight moon
the noonday sun

He'll rescue you
from random fate
restore your body
and your soul
He is with you
through birth and death
as you come in
and when you go

# 122

With joy I joined
a pilgrimage
to walk up to
Jerusalem
home of
the house
of God

Our feet stood at
the very gates
that welcomed
tribes of Israel
millennia ago

Jerusalem
above below
united whole
rebuilt with stones
that saw the thrones
of David's house
and witnessed justice
in the courts
of Solomon the wise

Lovers of Jerusalem
tranquility serenity
seek peace
within her palace walls
find armies of friends
at her gates

I speak for the sake
of brothers and foes
I speak for the sake of man
striving to live
at home with God
for the good of His house
for the good of us all

# 123

it's You I seek
when I gaze above
with pleading
slavegirl eyes

waiting for grace
trembling with fear
aware of where
power lies

mercy my God
have mercy on us

we've been forcefed
scorn and contempt
our spirit is broken
we're gagging
on bile
we're stuffed
and we're starved
and we're spent

peacocks in uniforms
cruel with pride
peck at what's left
of our souls

# 124

if You had not
been with us then
when we were prey

if You had not
been there to see
our enemies
prepare to eat us
swallow us
alive

then we would now
be air or water
overcome
dead souls
adrift

thank God
we're not

we slashed their nets
escaped their traps
and flew like birds
to live
and soar

thank God
who made
the earth and skies
bless God
who set us
free

# 125

those who trust in God
endure
like Zion
like Jerusalem
ringed by hills
forever there
to guard the
magnet core

those who trust in God
don't try
to grasp
the spears of fate
don't live at the edge
of a carousel
don't reach for
unholy grails

the center holds
it won't fly off
we're grounded
by our faith

Be good to the good
who trust You God
let evil go astray

may Israel
find peace endure
believe in You
and be secure

# 126

things were so bad
and then so good
we thought it all
a dream

we couldn't help
but smile throughout
when talked about
when word got out
when those who heard our story
couldn't help but see
the miracles
and say that God was good to us
and silently hope
He'd be good
to them too

all of us came back
by God
the stragglers
ingathered
mainstream

we carried
our burden
continued to sow
continued to hope
continued to know
that those who plant in tears
but plant
retain a chance
to harvest joy
and bring it home
and taste it

# 127

in vain
the grandest buildings are built
if there's no life
within

in vain
a fortune is guarded secure
if solely bequeathed
to a vault

in vain
a man may rise at dawn
to bake and bake
amassing bread
that surely will
decay

but sons and daughters
blessed by God
are gifts from God
and can propel
a legacy
of life
into the future

happy are they
who can bravely say
they toiled to nurture life
and aimed their arrows
far ahead
with steady hands
and hope

# 128

Happy are men
who think and act
with God in mind
they know when they're blessed

their wives are their homes
sweet grapes and wine
vineyards and groves
bearing fruit

daughters and sons
surround their table
saplings in fertile soil
branches that flower
arms that reach up
to gentle and generous skies

what life is richer
more pleasant than this

stay close to God
be blessed live well
and long enough to see
Jerusalem in peace
your children's children
at your feet

# 129

I've endured so much
from childhood on
I've been tested
again and again

I've been hit from all sides
furrowed and ploughed
but I am still here
now

I believe God is just
sees everything
that He knows
when and whom
to reward

no grass should thrive
in an evil field
no harvest should ever be
reaped
by those who oppress
may they wither
retreat
and never be
never be
blessed

# 130

I call to You
from the depths of me
I beg You
turn to me

Notice me
Hear me out
Judge me
leniently

I'm counting on
Your mercy
I am waiting
to be tried
No man can stand
before You
confident
of innocence

I wait like a tired
guard in the night
for relief to come with dawn
in darkness I wait
for a glimpse
of a ray
of Your
abundant light

# 131

I do not have
a haughty heart
my eyes do not
look down
I do not walk
in shoes too big
for me

when I can't have
what I desire
I can be weaned
of that desire
as a babe is weaned
from milk

but I cannot
be weaned
of dreams
I dream as Israel dreams
to be redeemed
from longing
to be close
to God again
intimate recipients
of milk and honey  now

# 132

Remember what I promised
when I suffered
through hard times
that I could never
close my eyes in peace
until I found
a place for You
a sacred holy space
where I could go
to find You
easily

Come with me friends
prepare yourselves
to be aware of truth
to bare your souls
to think to pray to feel
to talk to God
Who knows and hears
your every silent thought
to sense His omnipresence
always real

Remember what You promised
when You chose us chose our seed
to seek You and to learn
a way to live
You promised
if we followed You
You never would withdraw
You'd clothe our priests
in righteousness
You'd feed our needy bread
You'd crown our kings
until the end of days

# 133

O how good
how sweet to see
a dwelling place
of peace
brothers neighbors
living without strife

like oil that anoints
it sanctifies
like salve  like balm
it soothes

like morning dew
like fragrance rising
to perfume the air
like clouds that float
and bless the hills
of Zion

# 134

those who pray alone
unseen
in the foxholes of the night
mouthing silent holy words
of prayer
beseech and praise
the only God
who hears

bless God who made
the earth and sky
bless all who reach for Him
with open arms

# 135

Praise God  praise the idea of God
praise the name of God

willing servants of the Lord
standing up for Him
praise Him as they do His work
pleasantly they sing
that God is good to them
and finds them precious

I for one
know God
is greater than
all forces and all power
everything He wants to do
He can
sea and sky and earth and fire
thunder dew and zephyr
heed His word

it is God in charge of life
and God in charge of death
of firstborn sons of cattle and of kings

generations come and go
and God presides
eternally the judge
who can be bribed
with our repentance

gold and silver idols
blind to need and deaf to cries
are works of man
it's God who takes
and God who gives us
land and law and life

know Him bless Him
priests and servants
sing out Halleluya
to the One aware
of all the prayers
that saturate the air

# 136

Come give thanks
for God is good
and endlessly
He gives

Thank God the inconceivable
Creator of the skies
the One who set
the solid earth apart

Thank God the One
who rolled out suns
and planets moons and stars
and space and time
in webs of boundless night

Thank God who cares
remembered us
when we had reached the end
delivered us
with gentle arms
and hope

Thank God the One
who cut our chains
and plucked us up and out
of slavery and misery
and strongarmed the oppressors
who pursued us to the seas

Thank God who never
left our side
in desert wanderings
thank God
who keeps our enemies at bay

Thank God the One
providing bread
that keeps our flesh alive

Thank God
whose lovingkindness
has no end

# 137

homeless
we sit by the river and weep
remembering Zion
abandoning song
brazen
we balk as tormentors emerge
demanding performance and mirth
as we mourn

I'd rather be struck
dumb by a stroke
feel my right arm go limp
than lose my fragrant memories
of sweet Jerusalem
I long to rise to her in joy

my God
You hear them
taunting chanting
raze her raze her  raze
O to be the lucky man
who finds a way
to dash their plans
on unforgiving rock
so we can all return
and sing to You
again

# 138

I've come to search my soul and pray
and all that I feel
in my heart and my gut
is overwhelming gratitude

I need to bow
I need to kneel before You
prostrate myself on the ground
and weep
in thanks

I cried to You
You heard me
and You showered me with miracles
that drenched my world
and left me breathless
but alive
with newfound strength

earthly kings should sing to You
and listen for Your voice
how great to be able to hear the truth
and be deaf to the noise
of lies

I know if I seek You
You'll hear me  You're there
even when I am lost
I know there is nowhere
no battle no front
no place
where You
are not

# 139

God read my soul
and You will know
my core as You always have
and I never will  begin to know
the hows of all Your record keeping
but I am sure
as I am of my breath
that I have no thoughts
unknown to You
and that I can never
hide from You
How terrifying
comforting
and true

You can bring me back
from the edge of space
from the bottom of hell
and I won't know how
and I won't know why
but I have no doubt
that You can

Cover my night
with blankets of light
Enable me to see
Examine my soul
before You
exposed
Determine it worthy
to walk with You
to navigate my world

# 140

Shield me from
the evil souls
who lie in wait
to fight
like snakes
with pointed arrow
venom tongues
and eyes wide open
searching dirt
for naked heels to strike

and I am barefoot
sidestepping the coils

my gaze is down
my thoughts aloft
You are my only strength

Lure them into
pits of fire
from which they can't escape

so those whose eyes
look up to You
can walk the earth
and sing Your praise

# 141

Accept the prayers
from my mouth
like incense
like a sacrifice
smoke ascending
through a veil of clouds

Rain protection
on my soul
anoint my head
with holy oils
the guidance and the words
of righteous men

Let evil counsel
crash on rocks
distant from my path
an avalanche afar
that does no harm

I know, in time, my bones will lie
abandoned white as chalk
In time all flesh returns
to earth

yet I still need
to move  to breathe
and I still need to hope
and I still look to You
for life

# 142

I know You hear
my voice  my thoughts
the howling pain
within
when black moods come

I hide
but I have not a friend
who cares
to seek

I weep
You hear my tears
and as I live
and as I change
You are my constant
You remain

listen for the spark
within me
free it  lift me
rescue me
whirl me
out of shrouds
that now envelop me
enable me
to wear a crown
of righteousness
that fits

# 143

Hear me
Listen
Answer me
with mercy
as no human
can be guiltless
in Your court

an enemy attacked me
ground me down
to almost dead

my heart in shock
remembered days
when my thoughts
were of You
and my speech
was of miracles
wrought by Your hands
and my hands
reached for You
and my soul wanted drink
from the water of You
as a parched earth
thirsts

my breath is shallow
don't turn from me now
as my steps close in
to the grave
let morning come
with compassion from You
send currents of air
on which I'll soar
to safely land
on paths swept clean
of torturers and murderers

don't judge me now
just help me find a compass
that will lead me back
to You

# 144

Blessed is God
my rock my core
my guide in peace
my shield in war
my rescuer
my King

What am I
what's man to You
a shadow fleeting
passing through
beseeching You
beseeching You

Reach from heaven
rip the sky
move mountains  oceans
terrify
the hostile armies
liars  thieves
poised to strike and kill

Make them turn retreat and fall
I'll lift my lyre
and sing so all
can hear of peace
that will endure

O to live in lands of bounty
ruled by men of tolerance
youth surviving growing planting
harvesting their dreams
blessed are those
who live this way
and know that
God is King

# 145

I'll extol You endlessly
my God my Lord my King
and bless Your name
each day  each year
while there is breath
in me

Your sovereignty
extends to worlds
and generations
we can't know
but I have seen
Your miracles
and I will speak
and teach of You
ineffable in majesty
unreachable yet close enough
to intimately love

I have seen
Your kindness boundless
tolerance of man

we stoop and lean
we fall and cry
we look to You for food
and You
with open palms
provide
a niche for every soul

in time when air
is breathed in peace
when evil is expunged
all life will sing
and echo words of praise
now on my lips

# 146

as I inspire
as I expire
I sing my songs
to God

don't look for mortal
benefactors
destined as we all are
for the grave

fortunate are those
who seek support
from their Creator
from the One
who owns the earth
and air and water

the One
who metes out justice
feeds the starved
and frees the bonded
lifts the broken
loves the righteous
reaches out
to widows orphans
guides the weak
away from danger
and lets evil
self-destruct

generations
come and go
but God is King
eternally
sing Halleluya
praise His endless reign

# 147

it feels good to sing to God
our praise becomes Him

He who built Jerusalem
on high and here on earth
with golden light
and fragrant air
restorative to souls

He who knows the stars by name
each lost forgotten lonely star
each sun
He who lifts the humble
turns His back when wicked fall
Acknowledge Him
and answer
when He calls

He who turns the clouds
to fountains
making mountains
emerald green
sails the snowflakes
on the wind
to drape the hills in white

He who feeds the beast and raven
owns the bounty that we hunt
He who sends the arrows
and the hail

He who doesn't need our strength
but wants our love and fear
What man can stand alone
without His shield

Sing Halleluya  sing to God
Who gave us life
and laws of truth
How fortunate are we

# 148

Halleluya
from above
seraphim sing
where angels fly
in choruses of light

Halleluya over skies
where dazzling milky
constellations
flow through heaven's night

Halleluya
in their presence
praise the One
who made them

Halleluya
from below
where hellfires burn
and ice winds blow
at His command

Halleluya
from the deep
where oceans house
unknowns

Halleluya
from the hills
where trees bear fruit
for bird and beast

earthly lords and presidents
judges and celebrities
sages idols prodigies
commoners and kings
sing Halleluya in your sleep
and when you are awake
thank God for land you walk on
thank God for air you breathe
thank God whose banner
always waves
for human righteous deeds

# 149

Halleluya

sing to God
a different song
not just  help me God
when you are down

multitudes of righteous souls
look to Him
as life unfolds
rejoicing in ongoing gifts
of time

God gave us
bodies with our souls
hearts and guts
and flesh and bone
He must want us to sing
and love and dance and play
and live in ways
that honor Him
and bring us joy

when all pleasure
stems from power
grabbed or self-ordained
people fall
or even jump
from towers they have made

eternal laws
foresee the falls
and see the falls sustained
by justice
splendor of the wise
who reign with words
of God

# 150

Praise God's holiness
unknowable
Praise His deeds
magnificent
try to praise
what language
can't describe

Praise like a shofar
piercing the sky
Praise Him
with violins
Praise with your heart
Pound like a drum
Praise Him
with dancing limbs
Praise Him
with winds and bells and chimes
Praise Him
with prayers and dreams

Praise Him
with breath
that repeats like a song
like a psalm
each time
you breathe

In the end
what's left of me
may only be
a psalm

# Listing of Psalmsongs Based on Content*

Awe........................8, 19, 24, 29, 47, 48, 93, 97, 98, 104, 117, 144, 145, 147, 148

Beseeching God for mercy.....................................................36, 51, 106, 143

Blessings......45, 65, 67, 72, 103, 104, 110, 127, 128, 129, 133, 134, 144, 145

Closeness to God...............15, 16, 17, 23, 25, 26, 27, 42, 61, 63, 84, 86, 99, 101, 110, 118, 119, 131, 141

Evil (loss of faith in human behavior).........................12, 14, 28, 35, 53, 60, 94, 109, 137, 140

Faith and trust in God..................4, 5, 11, 14, 16, 18, 20, 23, 31, 34, 44, 54, 77, 82, 91, 121, 125, 139, 142

Fear of adversaries............................................................................3, 7, 57, 140

Fear of being abandoned by God..............................................10, 22, 71, 77, 88

Gratitude......................9, 21, 29, 30, 34, 40, 65, 66, 95, 96, 100, 107, 111, 113, 116, 118, 124, 136, 138

History and Torah (the Way of God)...............................44, 74, 78, 80, 81, 89, 95, 99, 105, 106, 114, 119, 122, 136, 137

Holiness....................................................................29, 87, 93, 98, 111, 132

Idols................................................................................................115, 135

Joy.............................................................1, 41, 84, 97, 112, 122, 127, 128, 133

Judgment.........................................................37, 43, 62, 72, 76, 130, 143

Lies and slander.................................................................52, 55, 58, 70, 109

Love....................................................................................................45, 80

Praise...........................................33, 47, 48, 81, 89, 92, 105, 135, 145, 146, 147, 148, 149, 150

| | |
|---|---|
| Remorse | 32, 38, 39, 51, 85, 90 |
| Revenge | 3, 11, 21, 35, 76, 83, 94, 109, 129, 140 |
| Reversal of fortune | 18, 21, 30, 34, 37, 40, 41, 46, 49, 64, 73, 75, 107, 113, 116, 126, 138 |
| Sabbath | 92 |
| Suffering | 6, 13, 56, 59, 69, 79, 88, 102, 120, 123, 129 |
| Truth | 1, 2, 15, 32, 49, 50, 62, 68, 78, 108, 119 |

*\* Please note that psalmsongs, as well as categories, can overlap in terms of content.*

# Index of First Lines

| | |
|---|---|
| Accept the prayers  from my mouth | 141 |
| Another song  a new one now | 98 |
| As I inspire  as I expire | 146 |
| Awesome Lord of all | 8 |
| Better men than I  know God is good | 73 |
| Blessed is God  my rock my core | 144 |
| Come give thanks  for God is good | 136 |
| Dear God  dear punishing God | 38 |
| Don't forget that  You chose us | 74 |
| Don't just think it | 100 |
| Don't make (me) believe | 102 |
| Don't pride yourself on all your wealth | 52 |
| Fight for me | 35 |
| First comes honesty  with self | 119 |
| Gather everyone  applaud | 47 |
| Give thanks to God  the source of good | 118 |
| God read my soul | 139 |
| God is King  He chose us | 99 |
| God is King  so earth be glad | 97 |
| God is known in Judah | 76 |
| God of vengeance God of right | 94 |
| God rules  behind the scenes | 93 |
| God said to you  sit on my right | 110 |
| God, with You lighting my way | 27 |
| God's power  immense | 48 |
| Great God speaks | 50 |
| Halleluya  worlds exist by the mercy | 106 |
| Halleluya  from above  seraphim sing | 148 |
| Halleluya  I will thank God | 111 |
| Halleluya  sing to God  a different song | 149 |
| Halleluya  think of God with gratitude | 113 |
| Happy are men  who think and act | 128 |
| Happy is he  who's afraid of God | 112 |
| Happy is he who knows | 41 |
| He sits hidden somewhere | 91 |
| Hear me  listen to my thoughts | 17 |
| Hear me  Listen  Answer me | 143 |
| Hear O Lord  as David sings | 61 |
| Help me God  I've lost my faith | 12 |
| Help me God before I drown | 69 |

| | |
|---|---|
| Homeless we sit by the river and weep | 137 |
| How can you be silent | 58 |
| How sweet it could be | 84 |
| I bring myself to You | 25 |
| I call to You from the depths of me | 130 |
| I cried by day at night I stood in prayer | 88 |
| I do not have a haughty heart | 131 |
| I knew Your will would be | 40 |
| I know my King | 18 |
| I know You hear my voice | 142 |
| I lift my eyes to mountains | 121 |
| I love that God will hear my voice | 116 |
| I proclaim You most high | 30 |
| I sing of the loving kindness | 89 |
| I still rely on You my God | 71 |
| I wanted to be mute | 39 |
| I will stay aware and thank You | 34 |
| I, mere king, hail You, my King | 21 |
| I'll extol You endlessly | 145 |
| I'm burdened trembling terrified | 55 |
| I'm calling You by name | 54 |
| I've come to search my soul and pray | 138 |
| I've endured so much | 129 |
| If You don't hear me | 28 |
| If You had not been with us then | 124 |
| In glory days and when in need | 108 |
| In God I trust | 11 |
| In God we trust | 82 |
| In silence the villain says to himself | 53 |
| In the worst of times | 46 |
| In vain the grandest buildings are built | 127 |
| Is this a test | 60 |
| It feels good to sing to God | 147 |
| It may look as though I'm mumbling | 64 |
| It's all God's | 24 |
| It's good to pause | 92 |
| It's You I seek when I gaze above | 123 |
| Judge me God of Israel | 72 |
| Just God Answer me when I call | 4 |
| Keep the blessings coming | 67 |
| Let's call to God when we're joyful | 95 |
| Like a parched doe | 42 |

| | |
|---|---|
| Listen to me  I am needy and bereft | 86 |
| Listen to this  rich man poor man | 49 |
| Look inside the me of me | 26 |
| Lord have mercy  take me in | 57 |
| Lucky is he who doesn't try to cover up  misdeed | 32 |
| My God  they've broken into  holy spaces | 79 |
| My God  my own exalted God | 109 |
| My tired body rises | 63 |
| No matter what  the state of your faith | 117 |
| Now is not the time | 83 |
| O God  I am overwhelmed | 3 |
| O God  I can't take this much longer | 13 |
| O God  don't leave me | 7 |
| O God don't punish me | 6 |
| O God have mercy | 56 |
| O how good  how sweet to see | 133 |
| O my God  I beg You | 5 |
| Only God  knows my silent self | 62 |
| Our ancestors and progeny | 90 |
| Pay attention to the truth | 78 |
| Praise God  praise the idea of God | 135 |
| Praise God's holiness  unknowable | 150 |
| Quickly come to me my God | 70 |
| Remember what I promised | 132 |
| Shepherd of Israel  You know love | 80 |
| Shield me from  the evil souls | 140 |
| Show clemency to me | 51 |
| Sing out to God | 33 |
| Sing to God  a different song | 96 |
| Sing to God  in joy and strength | 81 |
| So you never shine | 37 |
| Soul of mine  bless my God  Creator  boundless | 104 |
| Soul of mine  bless my God  and all He does | 103 |
| Stay close  You're mine | 16 |
| Stop the noise | 2 |
| Thank God in public | 105 |
| Thank You  God  thank You  God | 9 |
| The ink flows  from my soul to my pen | 45 |
| The sky tells Your story | 19 |
| They say God is dead | 14 |
| Things were so bad  and then so good | 126 |
| This is a song  from me to You | 101 |

| | |
|---|---|
| Those who pray alone | 134 |
| Those who trust in God | 125 |
| Throw me a rope | 59 |
| To not get lost | 1 |
| Voices from all corners of the earth | 66 |
| Wait for us | 65 |
| We who try to know You | 75 |
| We've heard we've learned from history | 44 |
| When God's presence is revealed | 68 |
| When holiness is the foundation | 87 |
| When I can't speak | 77 |
| When I lean on You | 31 |
| When I was down | 120 |
| When Israel escaped from Egypt | 114 |
| When sinning dictates | 36 |
| When times are hard | 20 |
| When you feel strong | 29 |
| When You show the watching world | 115 |
| Where are You when I need You | 10 |
| Who gets You good God | 15 |
| Why have You left me | 22 |
| With joy I joined a pilgrimage | 122 |
| You be my judge | 43 |
| You lead I'll follow | 23 |
| You wanted us home | 85 |
| You who have passed through narrow straits | 107 |